Ken Griffey, Jr.

THE HOME RUN KID

by
Larry Stone

SPORTS PUBLISHING INC.
www.SportsPublishingInc.com

Production manager: Susan M. McKinney
Cover design: Scot Muncaster
Photos: *The Associated Press,* Moeller High School

ISBN: 1-58261-041-x
Library of Congress Catalog Card Number: 99-61949

SPORTS PUBLISHING INC.
SportsPublishingInc.com

Printed in the United States.

CONTENTS

Ken Jr. and Ken Sr. are the only father and son to play together on a major league team. (AP/Wide World Photos)

CHAPTER ONE

Father and Son

Jubilation rocked the Seattle Mariner dugout, spurred by a moment that had never happened in baseball history, and may never again.

Ken Griffey Sr., a 40-year-old veteran, had hit a home run in the first inning off California Angels pitcher Kirk McCaskill. Then his son and teammate, 20-year-old budding superstar Ken Griffey Jr., stepped to the plate against McCaskill and hit another home run. Back-to-back homers by a father and son playing for the same team!

It was a magical moment that Mariner manager Jim Lefebvre said must have been scripted in Hollywood. In the dugout, Ken Sr. pumped his fist and said, "Yeah!"

It was September 14, 1990, and Griffey's teammates poured out of the dugout to high-five "Junior" as he crossed the plate. Young Griffey was looking for his father, who remained in the dugout, clapping his hands. After Junior descended the clubhouse steps, the two smiled at each other and embraced.

"It's about time," the senior Griffey told his son with a laugh.

The two had dreamed of this moment their entire lives. In 1987, when Junior began his professional career as the first pick in the entire amateur draft, his father told him, jokingly, that if he hurried through the Mariners' farm system, he'd try to hang on so they could play together.

That reality began to take form in late August 1990, when Griffey Sr., playing in his 18th major-league season, was released by the Cincinnati Reds and signed by the Mariners. On August 31, they played their first game together, becoming the only father and son ever to play together on the same team. The previous season, Junior's rookie year, they had become the first father-son combination to be active in the major leagues at the same time.

Before their first game together, against Kansas City at Seattle's Kingdome, Junior told the family's agent, Brian Goldberg, "It's really going to be weird tonight, playing with my dad."

Later, Goldberg drove to the park separately with Senior, who said, "You know, it's really going to be weird tonight, playing with my son."

It was weird, and highly emotional. Griffey Sr. started in left, Junior in center.

Ken and his dad played together for the first time professionally on August 31, 1990. (AP/Wide World Photos)

"This is the highlight of my career," Senior said. "I look over and that's my son in center field. I can't get used to it. It's an amazing feeling. It felt like we were back in the backyard, just playing catch. I kept thinking, 'I've changed his diapers.'"

Junior felt the same way. When the two trotted out to their positions in the first inning, he gave his father a quick wave, which he said was really a salute.

''I didn't know what to think," he said. "I wanted to cry or something. It just seemed like a father-son game, like we were out playing catch in the backyard."

Senior was so nervous that night he had difficulty concentrating, but in the bottom of the first inning, batting second, he ripped a single on the second pitch thrown to him by Royals starter Storm Davis. In so doing, he won a dinner bet he made

Ken Jr. uses the same style bat that his father used.
(AP/Wide World Photos)

with his son on who would get the first hit. It was the 2,091st hit of his career.

"The weird thing is," Junior said later, "all the guys are yelling, 'Let's go, Ken,' and I'm yelling, 'Let's go, Dad.'"

Junior then stepped to the plate, using the same style bat as his father, a black Louisville Slugger, 31 ounces, 34 inches. The only difference is that Junior's was inscribed "The Kid," his nickname. Junior also singled, his 275th career hit. Later in the game, Senior made a great defensive play, gunning down Bo Jackson, at the time the fastest player in baseball, at second base trying to stretch a single into a double. The play left Junior gawking in center, his glove over his mouth. "It runs in the family," he yelled over to his dad.

When the last out was made in the ninth inning, sealing a 5-2 Mariner victory, the father and son shared one more strong hug.

The rest of the season was one emotional highlight after another, topped by the back-to-back homers in Anaheim. In his month with the Mariners, Senior showed that their pairing was more than a publicity stunt, hitting .377 with three home runs and 18 runs batted in.

"The time I played with him was special," Senior said. "It was emotional for me. On the field, I was his teammate, off the field I was his father, and on the bench I was his coach."

It was the culmination of a father-son relationship forged from baseball.

CHAPTER TWO

Growing Up

Rusty Kuntz, a former Mariner outfield coach, once said, "If you could build a perfect player, it would be Ken Griffey Jr."

Ken, it seemed, was bred to play baseball. He was born November 21, 1969, in Donora, Pennsylvania, the same town that produced Hall of Famer Stan Musial. Ken was walking at seven months, the first sign that he had superior athletic genes. Those natural instincts were honed to superstar caliber by spending his entire life around the sport.

Ken's father was an All-State football player at Donora High School and planned on getting a college football scholarship. Griffey also was a baseball star, and when he was drafted in the 29th round of the June 1969 draft by the Cincinnati Reds, he signed a professional contract. He married his high school girlfriend, Alberta—known to all as Birdie —after graduation, and had just finished his first season with the Reds' rookie league team in Bradenton, Florida, when Ken Jr. was born.

Those early years were struggling ones for the Griffeys, who added another son, Craig, in 1971. Ken Sr. had to take jobs in the offseason to make ends meet, earning the minimum wage of $1.25 an hour in a print shop and later a steel mill. When he couldn't find work, the family accepted welfare.

"Junior has always thought of himself as a big-leaguer because that's all he remembers," Senior said.

"He doesn't remember Bradenton, Sioux Falls (Iowa), Tampa or Three Rivers (Quebec)."

Those tough early years for the Griffeys, wandering around the backroads of the minor leagues, changed dramatically in 1973, when Ken Sr. made the Reds and settled the family in Cincinnati. By 1975, he was a starting outfielder for the "Big Red Machine," one of the most powerful teams in baseball history.

With a lineup that included Hall of Famers Johnny Bench and Joe Morgan, all-time hits leader Pete Rose, and RBI machine Tony Perez, they won the World Series in 1975 and 1976. Griffey was a big part of the Big Red Machine, making the All-Star team in 1976, 1977 and 1980 and being named the game's MVP in 1980, when he went 2-for-3 with a home run. In 1976, he batted .336 and was the runnerup for the batting title.

Ken clowns around with his high school baseball coach. (Moeller High School)

Ken and his assistant coach at Moeller High School. (Moeller High School)

By the time his career ended in 1991, after playing one more injury-riddled season with his son in Seattle, Griffey Sr. had accumulated 2,143 hits and a lifetime batting average of .296.

Junior soaked up the baseball atmosphere, often taking batting practice against his dad before home games at the Reds' Riverfront Stadium. Many of his friends were the sons of other Reds players. He especially loved the annual father-son games, when he would get dressed in his uniform hours before it was time to leave for the ballpark. Yet he says he didn't think of his father as a baseball star, but just a normal father who happened to make his living as a baseball player. Griffey Sr.'s own father, Buddy, abandoned the family when Senior was just 2, and he promised that he would be a good father to his own kids. The Griffeys remain an extremely close family to this day.

Growing up, Ken dominated the youth leagues in which he played. (AP/Wide World Photos)

"I didn't want Junior to go through the same thing in life," he said.

Meanwhile, Junior was starting his own career in the youth leagues of Cincinnati. He was so dominant as a youngster that his mother had to take his birth certificate to games because opponents couldn't believe he wasn't older. According to Birdie, Junior didn't make an out in an organized game until he was 15 years old. He was so upset he told his mom he wanted to quit.

"Why are you so upset?" she said. "Your dad makes outs all the time."

"I'm not my dad," Junior replied. "I don't make outs."

In 1981, when Junior was just 11, his father was traded to the New York Yankees. The family decided that while Ken Sr. lived in New York during the season, the kids would remain in Cincinnati with Birdie. Just as Junior was hitting adolescence and his baseball skills were beginning to blossom, his father was usually not around to watch.

Senior tried to stay connected to his son as much as possible, however. During spring training, Ken Jr. and Craig would go to Florida each year for special tutoring. Junior made frequent trips to New York, where his father would pitch him batting practice at Yankee Stadium. Even at age 12, Junior rarely struck out.

"He threw curves, sliders, everything," Junior said. "It's a confidence builder when you can hit against your dad."

After one Yankee game, which they lost, Junior was running around a corridor outside the clubhouse playing with several other sons of Yankee players. The Yankee manager, Billy Martin, still upset by the defeat, became angry at the youngsters, and singled out Junior and Craig, telling Ken Sr. to never bring them to the clubhouse again. The incident

Junior played baseball and football at Moeller High School in Cincinnati. (Moeller High School)

has stuck with Junior over the years, and he has always said he will never play for the Yankees.

When Junior entered Cincinnati's Moeller High School, he was a baseball and football star. He played wide receiver on Moeller's state championship football team as a junior, but was academically ineligible as a senior. It was clear from the start that his future was as a baseball player.

At Moeller, the same school that produced major leaguer stars Barry Larkin and Buddy Bell, he set records with three homers in a game, 11 home runs in a season and 20 in his career. Major league scouts flooded Moeller's games to see the 6-foot-3, 195-pound teenager with superior speed and a rifle arm. Atlanta Braves general manager Bobby Cox (now the team's manager) said Ken Jr. was the best prospect he had ever seen. The Mariner scouts agreed.

Oddly enough, the only time Junior struggled was on the rare occasions that his father was able to break away from his team to watch him play.

"Only when his father was there would Kenny pressure himself," his high school coach, Mike Cameron, once said. "A hundred scouts could be in the stands, and it wouldn't make a difference."

Ken said that when his father was present, it was the only time he felt he had to impress someone. His father told him, "I'm the one guy you don't have to impress."

Ken and his family decided he would accept a scholarship to the University of Oklahoma if he wasn't picked in the first three rounds of the draft in his senior year. If baseball didn't work out, he planned to study mechanical drawing and become an architect. That remains an interest to this day, and he even helped design his family's home in Orlando, Florida.

Ken and two of his high school teammates take time to pose for a photo. (Moeller High School)

He need not have worried about not being picked high in the draft. The Mariners scouts have a rating system for their prospects in which 50 to 59 means the player has the potential to be an All-Star. All five scouts who saw Ken scored him between 63 and 73—superstar caliber.

On June 2, 1987, the 17-year-old Ken, who hit .422 his senior year at Moeller, was picked No. 1 overall by the Mariners, the first of 1,263 players chosen that year. He quickly signed a contract that gave him a $180,000 bonus, and reported immediately to the Mariners' rookie league team in Bellingham, Washington.

The Kid was on his way.

3

Minor Leagues

It was only fitting that Ken's first hit as a professional was a home run. His minor-league career was a fleeting one, as it was abundantly clear to all who saw him play, even as a 17-year-old, that he was on the fast track to the major leagues.

Wearing No. 24 in honor not of Willie Mays, the Hall of Fame outfielder with whom he is constantly compared, but rather Rickey Henderson, his boyhood idol, Ken wound up hitting .313 with 14 homers and 40 RBIs in 54 games for Bellingham.

He did go into a slump early in the season, watching his average drop to .230. Homesick, he called his mom for help. Birdie flew west as quickly as she could make the arrangements and gave Junior a dose of tough love.

"I knew he needed some sympathy," she said. "But I got mad and told him to concentrate on his career. He didn't call me for four days."

Birdie's advice worked. Junior hit .450 the rest of the season and was voted the Northwest League's top prospect. Still, playing in remote Bellingham, located about 90 miles north of Seattle and 20 miles south of the Canadian border, was a culture shock for Ken. Their road trips, some as long as 10 hours on a 1958 bus that wasn't equipped with a restroom, were difficult. Ken sometimes slept in the overhead luggage compartment.

"To be perfectly honest with you, it was a whole lot worse than I ever imagined," he told a reporter.

Ken was struggling in other ways. He had a serious conflict with the teenaged sons of the team's bus driver. One allegedly called him a racial epithet, while the other allegedly came after him with a gun.

"I was really upset, mad," Griffey told the *Seattle Times*. "Growing up back home, I never had to deal with anything like that."

Years later, Ken made a shocking revelation. When he came home to Cincinnati after the season, he swallowed 277 aspirin and wound up in intensive care at the hospital.

"It seemed like everyone was yelling at me in baseball, then I came home and everyone was yelling at me there," Ken told the *Seattle Times*. "I got depressed. I got angry."

Ken said he decided to make the story public to help teens. "Don't ever try to commit suicide," he said. "I'm living proof how stupid it is."

Ken said the incident helped strengthen his relationship with his father. It did little to dim his playing career. The next season, in 1988, he started out at single-A San Bernardino, California, where each time he came to the plate, the public address announcer would ask, "What time is it?" The crowd would yell, "Griffey time!"

It was Griffey time. Although he spent two months on the disabled list with a strained back, he hit .338 for San Bernardino and was promoted to Double-A Vermont when he was healthy again in mid-August. When he finished out the season playing 10 games there, Ken's brief minor-league career was over.

The big leagues were beckoning.

Rookie Growing Pains

Near the end of spring training in 1989, just before the Mariners were about to board a bus for an exhibition game with the Cubs in Mesa, Arizona, Seattle manager Jim Lefebvre called Ken into his office. The 19-year-old youngster had performed sensationally all spring, but Lefebvre's serious demeanor had Ken worried, even more so when the manager began to talk.

Ken, who had boldly predicted before camp even began that he would make Seattle's final roster, couldn't believe it when Lefebvre began telling

At 19, Ken predicted he would make the Mariners' roster out of spring training. (AP/Wide World Photos)

Junior signs autographs for fans during spring training in Arizona. (AP/Wide World Photos)

him what a difficult decision he had to make, and how he had discussed it with his coaches before making the agonizing choice.

By now, Ken was completely convinced he was going back to the minors. Then Lefebvre smiled and ended the prank.

"Congratulations," he told Ken. "You've made the team. You're my starting centerfielder."

"My heart started ticking again," a relieved Ken said later. "Those were probably the best words I've ever heard."

Ken had given the Mariners no choice, really. He hit in 15 straight Cactus League games, setting Seattle spring-training records for hits (32), total bases (49) and RBI (20) while hitting .359. Skeptics had predicted that his hitting would tail off as pitchers rounded into shape, but it just got better. About the only rough spot for him that spring came when he was playing catch on the first day of training camp, and the ball skipped off his glove and hit him squarely in his right eye, knocking him out of that day's workout.

"They told me he could hit, he could run and he could throw," Lefebvre said with a laugh. "But no one told me he couldn't play catch."

The tremendous promise that Griffey carried from the day the Mariners drafted him was starting to be realized. Actually, many in the Seattle organization had felt it would be best for Griffey, with just 129 minor-league games behind him (all but 17 at Single A, the lowest professional rung), to start the season in the minor leagues at Triple-A, or even Double A. His spring training play had made it abundantly clear he was ready for the major leagues — both physically and mentally. He handled himself like a veteran, which is how he felt about himself.

"Man, this is my 12th spring training camp," he said. "That's 10 with my dad and two on my own."

It wasn't all smooth for Griffey that spring, however. At the beginning, some of his teammates razzed him about his age, calling him "Wonder Boy" and teasing him that he was only in camp because of his father. He finally became upset enough to go to his manager. Lefebvre told him if he wasn't tough enough to handle the other players, perhaps he should start the year in the minors. Ken didn't complain again, and as his play improved, the ribbing gradually stopped.

Ken had extra motivation to make the team that spring. He knew that his father, pushing age 40 and back in the Reds camp, didn't have many more years to play. If they were to realize the family dream of playing in the majors at the same time, Ken Jr. needed to hurry to the big leagues. The day

Ken played his first major-league game against the Oakland A's on April 4, 1989. (AP/Wide World Photos)

after the Mariners announced that Junior would be their starting center fielder, Ken Sr. signed a one-year contract with the Cincinnati Reds. It was official—they would be the first father-son combination in major-league history to play in the same season. When Junior called his dad to tell him he had made the Mariners, Ken Sr. was stunned.

"I kept saying, 'Dad? Dad? Dad?'" Junior recalled. "He didn't say anything."

Ken's first major-league game was at the Oakland Coliseum against the A's on April 4, 1989, facing their ace pitcher, Dave Stewart. Junior was the youngest player in the majors. In his first at-bat, he hammered a double off Stewart on the second pitch thrown to him. A week later, in his first home game at the Kingdome—on his father's 39th birthday—he homered on the first pitch from the Chicago White Sox' Eric King. Later in the season, in his first pinch-hitting appearance, he hit a two-run

*Junior is famous for his sensational defensive plays,
such as this diving catch. (AP/Wide World Photos)*

home run off Milwaukee's Bill Wegman to win a game for Seattle. On Ken Griffey Jr. Poster Day, June 4, he hit a game-winning home run off knuckle-baller Charlie Hough, whom he had never faced.

There were also struggles and growing pains. After that double off Stewart, Ken went hitless in his next 18 at-bats. On April 22, he was batting .189 (10-for-53) and starting to get down on himself. Lefebvre dropped him from No. 2 to No. 6 in the Mariners' batting order.

"That was a big moment for him," said teammate Jeffrey Leonard. "When you're down like that, you can go one of two ways. He could have ended up back in Calgary. See how he responded."

He responded with 13 hits in his next 16 at-bats, a stretch that resulted in his being named American League player of the week. In the week, he had eight straight hits and reached base 11 consecutive times, batting .516. He also turned in the first of what would be a career-long catalog of sensational defensive plays that would make highlight videos and stun teammates and opponents alike. In a game against Detroit, with the Mariners leading 5-3 in the eighth, Ken raced to the wall in left center to haul in a line drive by Fred Lynn with runners on first and second. Then he whirled around and fired a perfect throw to third base to cut down Lou Whitaker, who was trying to advance after the catch.

"It was a spectacular play at a spectacular moment," Lefebvre said.

Ken became so popular in Seattle that a local company marketed a Ken Griffey Jr. chocolate bar, and they sold 800,000 of them. The teenaged Ken couldn't eat his own candy bar. They made his face break out.

With his batting average hovering around .300 through July, Ken was the overwhelming favorite to win the Rookie of the Year award—until he slipped in the shower and broke his hand, putting him on the disabled list for nearly a month. Ken returned to the lineup on August 21, but struggled the rest of the season, batting .181 in the final month. He admitted he was trying too hard to make up for the time he had lost. He ended up hitting .264 with 16 homers (just three after the All-Star break), 61 RBI, and 16 stolen bases. He finished third in the rookie balloting.

"Every day, he shows you something that tells you he's going to be an incredible player," Lefebvre said.

Not bad for a 19-year-old kid who was barely two years out of high school. What the season showed, however, was that Ken had barely scratched the surface of his ability.

Blossoming into Stardom

Lefebvre called Ken "a comet shooting across the sky," and he soon soared to the upper regions of baseball's galaxy.

In 1990, rather than falling victim to baseball's supposed "sophomore jinx," Ken hit .300 with 22 homers, and became the first Mariner ever voted into the starting lineup of the All-Star game. At age 20, he was the second-youngest player ever to start the mid-summer classic. It would become a familiar result—Ken has been voted an outfield starter every year through 1998.

Junior waves to the crowd while accepting an award at the Kingdome. (AP/Wide World Photos)

Ken received more than two million All-Star votes in 1990. (AP/Wide World Photos)

Ken supporters in 1990—more than two million of whom cast votes for him—were no doubt thinking of plays like the one he made in April at Yankee Stadium, where he made a leaping catch at the wall to rob Jesse Barfield of his 200th career home run. Ken, who that year was voted the first of his eight Gold Gloves for fielding excellence, has made dozens of spectacular catches in his career, but the Barfield play is universally ranked as one of his very best. Ken himself has always considered his best catch to be the one he made in 1991, when he slammed into the Kingdome wall to take away an extra-base hit from Texas' Ruben Sierra.

Dazzling plays like that, coupled with Ken's charisma and constant smile, were quickly making him one of baseball's most popular players. His Mariner teammate, catcher Dave Valle, called Ken the Michael Jordan of baseball. Fans clearly agreed, making him the American League's top All-Star vote

Ken always seems to have fun while playing baseball. (AP/Wide World Photos)

getter in 1991, when Ken hit .327 with 22 homers and 100 RBI.

Another teammate, veteran relief pitcher Goose Gossage, said: "If there was another league, he'd be in it. And he'd be the only one there." Joe Morgan, who played with Ken's father in Cincinnati, said that Junior would be the player he would take first if he was starting a team.

"Like Willie Mays, Junior has no limitations on the field," Morgan said. "He's as good defensively as he is in the batter's box. A lot of guys can hit, but most of them don't want to play defense. And Junior enjoys the game like Willie Mays did. He seems to have fun, and that's what the game is all about."

Over the years, in fact, some have criticized Ken for being too carefree. In 1991, a Seattle columnist wrote him an open letter questioning his effort and work habits, asking, "We wonder if you

Junior was named MVP of the 1992 All-Star Game.
(AP/Wide World Photos)

are going to settle for being good, when you have the skills to be one of the greatest." Ken admitted the article forced him to soul-search about his goals.

"It was a bad article, but it came out good because it made me think about the person I want to be and what I can accomplish in this game," he said. "My intensity is always there, but when I step in there, to the plate, maybe it doesn't always show. I want to be the best player I can be. It may seem I'm being selfish, but if I am, it's for the good of the team."

In 1994, New York Yankees manager Buck Showalter blasted Ken for "disrespecting" the game. In particular, he criticized Ken for not tucking in his jersey and for his trademark style of wearing his cap backwards during warmups. Ken explained that his hat mannerism dates back to his youth, when he used to don his father's baseball caps. They were so big they fell over his eyes, so in order to see he turned it backwards. Besides, Ken said, "He said I don't take the game seriously. What's not serious about my numbers the last six years?" His Mariner teammates showed their support the next time the Mariners played the Yankees. When they came out for pre-game exercises, all wore their hats backwards.

Ken Sr., who had been limited to just 30 games in 1991 because of a neck injury he suffered in a car accident, finally retired from baseball after the season. He remained as hitting coach in 1992 and Junior produced a .308 average with 27 homers and 103 RBIs. He experienced one of his career highlights when he was voted the MVP of the All-Star Game in San Diego, where he homered (off Greg Maddux), singled and doubled in three at-bats. This was particularly special to Ken because his father had earned the same honor 12 years earlier.

"It means a lot, knowing he played in the All-Star Game and homered, too," Junior said. "It's not like I wanted to duplicate what he did—I just wanted to have fun."

Another highlight for Ken that year occurred when he married the former Melissa Gay, whom he had met when she asked him to dance at an alcohol-free under-21 club when both were 19. The two were made for each other. She is also athletic, and they love to participate together in such varied activities as jet skiing, paint ball, four wheeling, roller blading and golf.

The following year, 1993, saw Ken blossom as a home-run hitter. Over a nine-day span from July 20 to 28, he homered in eight consecutive games, tying a major-league record. The streak finally ended before a near sellout crowd at the Kingdome. "If he had hit a home run in his last at-bat," Mariner pitcher Erik Hanson said, "the roof would have come off, and we'd have an outdoor stadium."

Ken showed his tremendous power that year at the All-Star game in Baltimore's Camden Yards. During the Home Run Derby, he became the first player to ever hit the B&O warehouse beyond the right-field stands. Ken finished the season with 45 home runs to go along with a .309 batting average and 109 RBIs.

Before the 1994 season, Ken went to longtime Mariner announcer Dave Niehaus to request that Niehaus stop calling him The Kid. After all, Ken now had a kid of his own, Trey Kenneth Griffey, born in January. After the birth, as a joke, Mariner general manager Woody Woodward sent the Griffeys a signed Mariner contract, dated 2012. The Griffeys had their second child in October of 1995, a daughter, Taryn.

Junior got another huge thrill in 1994, when his brother Craig, who had signed as a minor-league outfielder with the Mariners after a football career as a defensive back at Ohio State University, started in left field alongside Ken in a spring training game in Arizona. It was the first time they had played on the same team since 1981, when Ken was 12 and Craig was 10. To Ken, it ranked right up there with his experience playing next to his father in 1990.

The nickname change highlighted the fact that Ken had fully matured as a player. For the first time (but certainly not the last), he put forth a challenge to Roger Maris' cherished record of 61 home runs in a season. Through May, Ken had 22 homers, breaking Mickey Mantle's record of 20 in 1956. He also broke Babe Ruth's 66-year-old record for home runs through June, slugging 32. He made the All-Star team with a record 6,079,688 votes.

It was the wrong year to have a record-challenging season. The major-league players went on strike August 11 and didn't return. The remainder of the season, including the World Series, was canceled. Ken, who hit a grand slam against Oakland in the team's final game, wound up with 40 home runs in the 112 games that were played — 50 short of a full season. He was on pace to hit 58 homers and would have joined several players who seemed ready to challenge the record.

"It might have been something to see," he said after the strike ended. "We had four of us in there, Frank (Thomas), (Matt) Williams and (Jeff) Bagwell. Or five: Barry (Bonds) was getting hot. Or even six: Albert Belle was hot, too. We might have pushed one another to a record. Now, we'll never know."

By this time, Ken had become a cultural phenomenon. He was featured in his own video game, made a cameo appearance in the movie "Little Big League," appeared in an episode of "The Fresh Prince," ran for president as part of an ad campaign, and became partners with other superstar athletes in a restaurant chain.

Less public has been his generosity in charitable ventures, particularly those involving kids. He is heavily involved in the Make-A-Wish Foundation and has never turned down a request from the organization, which grants wishes made by seriously ill children. He received the 1994 Recognition Award from the Make-A-Wish foundation, and also received the A. Bartlett Giamatti Award from the Baseball Assistance Team for his work with senior citizens, focusing on former Negro League players.

He said that his main regret of the strike was that the Mariners, who had won six straight games when the games were halted, wouldn't have a chance to continue their playoff drive. By now a full-blown superstar, the big void in Griffey's career was the fact that the Mariners still hadn't qualified for postseason play.

That was about to change.

Ken works with numerous charities, especially those focusing on kids. (AP/Wide World Photos)

Making the Playoffs

Ken led off first base, ready to run faster than he ever had in his life. It was the bottom of the 11th inning in the fifth and deciding game of the 1995 American League Divisional Series. The Mariners trailed the New York Yankees, 5-4. Joey Cora was running at third base, and batting champion Edgar Martinez was at the plate.

Crack! Martinez lined the ball into the left-field corner, and Ken took off. Cora scored easily, tying the game, but could Ken get around the bases to give Seattle the victory? The sellout crowd at the

The Mariners celebrate their win over the Yankees in the final game of their 1995 division series. (AP/Wide World Photos)

Kingdome leapt to their feet, cheering him on. As Ken rounded second, he was focused on one person: third-base coach Sam Perlozzo. Perlozzo frantically waved him home. Ken didn't break stride around third and sprinted for the plate. Yankee leftfielder Gerald Williams, meanwhile, had tracked down the ball and thrown to Yankee shortstop Tony Fernandez, who fired to catcher Jim Leyritz. But Ken slid safely into home plate, giving the Mariners the victory. They would be playing the Cleveland Indians for the American League pennant!

Ken's game-winning run set off a wild celebration. Perlozzo jumped in the air so intensely he strained a calf muscle. Ken was buried by his teammates. "This," he said, "is where I always wanted to be. This, more than anything."

Besides playing next to his dad, it was Ken's greatest moment in baseball. It culminated a magical, breakthrough season for Ken and the Mariners that at one point seemed destined for heartache.

On May 26, while making one of the best catches of his career, Ken broke his left wrist. He slammed into the Kingdome wall to snare a drive off the bat of Baltimore's Kevin Bass. Somehow, he managed to hold onto the ball despite impact so great that the pad on the fence was still dented with the imprint of his body the next day. Manager Lou Piniella called it the best catch he had ever seen. It was a costly one for the Mariners, and frightening for Ken, who knew instantly the injury was serious. His first question for the doctor was whether he would play again.

It turned out the wrist was broken in 15 places, and during surgery seven screws and a metal plate were inserted to stabilize the wrist. Ken not only played again, but much more quickly than doctors anticipated. They thought he would be out for three months, but he returned several weeks early, on August 15.

Without Ken's presence for 73 games, the Mariners seemed destined for another disappointing season, and the potential cost was great. The franchise had begun play as an expansion team in 1977 and didn't have its first winning season until 1991. There was talk that if the city voters didn't authorize funding for a new stadium, the team would have to move out of Seattle. The pressure to make the playoffs was immense, but while Ken was out with his broken wrist, the Mariners dropped from 2 1/2 to 11 1/2 games behind the Angels in the AL West.

After his return, Ken struggled, hitting only .255 with 10 homers and 27 RBI in 45 games. His presence alone seemed to inspire the team, which adopted the slogan Refuse to Lose. After compiling a 3-6 record in Junior's first nine games, they took off. Many believe the key game of the season was a victory over the Yankees on August 24, in which Ken hit a two-run, game-winning homer off John Wetteland in the ninth inning. After trailing the Angels by as many as 13 games, the Mariners made one of the greatest comebacks in baseball history to finish the regular season tied for the division title. In a one-game playoff at the Kingdome, behind a brilliant pitching performance from Randy Johnson, they beat the Angels 9-1 to advance to the playoffs.

Ken was superb against the Yankees, hitting five home runs to tie Reggie Jackson's record for most home runs in one five-game playoff series. In the clinching game, he set the stage for his 11th-inning trip around the bases with an upper-deck homer off David Cone in the eighth inning that helped Seattle erase a 4-2 Yankee lead.

The Mariners went on to lose the AL pennant to the Indians in six games, keeping them out of the World Series. They got a sweet victory after the season when the state legislature approved funding for the stadium that would keep the Mariners in Seattle. Set to open in July of 1999, the ballpark has been dubbed by some "The House that Griffey Built."

CHAPTER SEVEN

MVP And Beyond

Unbelievably, it happened to Ken again in 1996 — another broken bone in his hand, another scary wait to see if he would come back from the injury the same player as before.

This time, he broke the hamate bone in his right hand while checking a swing on June 20. Doctors removed the bone, but first they had to move the nerves, a procedure that caused loss of feeling in his pinky, and occassionally through his entire right hand.

Ken soon proved that he was still a fearsome slugger. Despite missing 20 games after the operation, he still hit 49 home runs and drove in 139 runs, astounding teammates.

"You don't come back from that surgery in a couple of weeks and hit 50 home runs," said third baseman Dave Hollins, who had the same surgery on both hands. "At least you don't if you're human."

Ken's great season spawned a fierce debate about who was the Mariners' Most Valuable Player, Griffey or shortstop Alex Rodriguez, the 21-year-old sensation who led the league with a .358 average and had 36 homers and 123 RBI. Rodriguez himself said late in the season, "Junior's the MVP, period." Ken wound up finishing fourth in the balloting, but he got first-place votes from both Seattle writers, controversially preventing Rodriguez from getting the award. It went instead to outfielder Juan Gonzalez of the Texas Rangers, the team that had edged out Seattle for the AL West title.

In 1997, Ken finally made it through the entire season healthy, and the result was an assault on Maris' home run record that riveted the nation. He hit two homers against the Yankees on Opening Night, set a record with 24 homers through May, and hit No. 30 on July 5.

Ken made the All-Star team as the leading vote-getter for the fourth time, but at the All-Star Game in Cleveland, where reporters were clamoring to know if he could break Maris' record, he used the opportunity to get something off his chest.

"As best I can tell, I'm well-liked," he said. "But I'm simply not respected as someone who goes out every day and gives the best I can for my team."

Ken slowed down measurably after the All-Star break, hitting just two more homers in July. In one stretch, he went 60 at-bats between home runs. The slowdown perplexed Mariner fans, but Ken finally revealed that his play was adversely affected by the death of his 54-year-old mother-in-law on July 10 from congestive heart failure. He was also hampered by a hamstring injury.

"I'd only experienced one other death in the family that was so close," he told a reporter. "I was worried about how my wife and kids would react. They hung in a lot better than I did because I was just in a fog for awhile."

Ken rebounded to hit .330 with a dozen homers in August and finished with his greatest season yet, and one of the best in history. He hit 56 homers, tied for the seventh-most ever, and drove in 147 runs, most in the majors. He hit .304 and led the league in nine offensive categories. At the end of the season, he was the unanimous choice as American League MVP, just the 13th player in history to receive all first-place votes.

"I am without a doubt the happiest old man in the world," his father said. "Winning the MVP is a special thing. I know how special because I tried with all my might and ability to be worthy of one."

Ultimately, the season was a disappointment for Ken. While the Mariners won the AL West title for the second time in three years, they were eliminated in the first round of the playoffs by the Baltimore Orioles. Ken, who always says his No. 1 goal in baseball is to earn a World Series ring like this father (who has three), had just two singles in 15 at-bats in the playoffs.

"All I've ever wanted to do here is win," Ken said. "I've done a few things in this game that my father didn't, but he's got those rings. I don't. But I'm going to get one."

Ken showed at the end of the season that the team meant more to him than his personal glory. On the final weekend of the season, when he still had an outside shot at Maris' record, he sat out a game against Oakland so that he could rest for the playoffs.

In 1998, Ken once again stalked Maris, which created an uncomfortable atmosphere for him. He dislikes talking about himself, particularly about hitting home runs and the home-run chase, which he has long claimed is not important to him.

"The record's not important," he said. "What's important is getting the trophy with all the flags on it. The fans may not understand it, but that's the way it is. It's a team. It's not a one-man show."

Though he fell short of the heights scaled by Mark McGwire and Sammy Sosa in 1998, Griffey had another remarkable season. He matched his 1997 total with 56 homers while driving in 146 runs. Once again, one slow power stretch wiped out his chance of surpassing Maris. On July 10, he was tied with McGwire with 37 homers, but he hit only two in a month-long stretch from July 14 to August 15.

Ken hit 56 homers in 1997 and again in 1998.
(AP/Wide World Photos)

Ken won the home-run hitting contest at the All-Star Game in Denver, but only after changing his mind about sitting out the contest. That decision had been very unpopular in Denver, where there was great anticipation for Griffey to compete against McGwire in the home-run derby. Ken reconsidered after receiving thunderous boos during batting practice and when he received his trophy as the top vote-getter.

"I don't like to get booed," he said. "I don't think anyone does. This is not a time to get booed, at an All-Star Game. And, you know, if they want to see me in the home-run competition, the fans, there's 4 million reasons why I did it, for them."

Still only 28 years old after the 1998 season, Ken should have many huge achievements ahead of him. Hank Aaron believes that Ken is the top candidate to surpass Aaron's record of 755 career home runs. He is the youngest player ever to reach

350 homers, and fourth-youngest player to reach 1,000 RBIs.

Typically, Ken puts his career goals in a family perspective.

"I think of 19 years," he said. "My dad played 19 years, and all I want is to have as good a career as he did."

He seems well on his way to reaching that goal.

Ken Griffey, Jr. Quick Facts

Full Name:	George Kenneth Griffey, Jr.
Team:	Seattle Mariners
Hometown:	Donora, Pennsylvania
Position:	Centerfielder
Jersey Number:	24
Bats:	Left
Throws:	Left
Height:	6-3
Weight:	205 pounds
Birthdate:	November 21, 1969

1998 Highlight: Hit 56 home runs for the second consecutive season.

Stats Spotlight: A 50-homer season in 1999 would give Griffey 400 for his career.

Little-Known Fact: On August 31, 1990, Ken Griffey, Sr. and Ken Griffey, Jr. become the first father-son tandem to play in the same Major League Baseball game.

Ken Griffey Jr's Professional Career

Year	Club	AVG	G	AB	R	H	2B	3B	HR	RBI	BB	SO	SB
1989	Seattle	.264	127	455	61	120	23	0	16	61	44	83	16
1990	Seattle	.300	155	597	91	179	28	7	22	80	63	81	16
1991	Seattle	.327	154	548	76	179	42	1	22	100	71	82	18
1992	Seattle	.308	142	565	83	174	39	4	27	103	44	67	10
1993	Seattle	.309	156	582	113	180	38	3	45	109	96	91	17
1994	Seattle	.323	111	433	94	140	24	4	40*	90	56	73	11
1995	Seattle	.258	72	260	52	67	7	0	17	42	52	53	4
1996	Seattle	.303	140	545	125	165	26	2	49	140	78	104	16
1997	Seattle	.304	157	608	125*	185	34	3	56*	147*	76	121	15
1998	Seattle	.284	161	633	120	180	33	3	56*	146	76	121	20

M.L. Totals   .300 1375 5226 940 1569 294   27 350 1018 656 876 143

*Indicates League Leader

Active Career Batting Leaders

1. Tony Gwynn .339

2. Mike Piazza .333

3. Wade Boggs .329

4. Frank Thomas .321

5. Edgar Martinez .318

6. Alex Rodriguez .313

7. Kenny Lofton .311

8. Rusty Greer .310

9. Mark Grace .310

10. Nomar Garciaparra .309

25. Ken Griffey, Jr. .300

***Ken helps break ground for the Mariners' new stadium.
(AP/Wide World Photos)***

Active Career AB/HR

Mark McGwire	11.2
Juan Gonzalez	14.2
Albert Belle	14.6
Ken Griffey, Jr.	**14.9**
Jose Canseco	15.2

Heading into 1999, Ken was seventh on the list of active career home run leaders. (AP/Wide World Photos)

Active Career Home Run Leaders

1.	Mark McGwire	457
2.	Barry Bonds	411
3.	Jose Canseco	397
4.	Cal Ripken	384
5.	Fred McGriff	358
6.	Gary Gaetti	351
7.	**Ken Griffey, Jr.**	**350**
8.	Harold Baines	348
9.	Darryl Strawberry	332
10.	Andres Galarraga	332

Active Career RBI leaders

1.	Cal Ripken	1514
2.	Harold Baines	1480
3.	Gary Gaetti	1294
4.	Chili Davis	1294
5.	Barry Bonds	1216
6.	Jose Canseco	1214
7.	Andres Galarraga	1172
8.	Mark McGwire	1130
9.	Bobby Bonilla	1106
10.	Will Clark	1106
16.	**Ken Griffey, Jr.**	**1018**

Ken watches another home run leave the ballpark.
(AP/Wide World Photos)

Ken is congratulated by teammates Alex Rodriguez and David Segui (left) after one of his league-leading 56 home runs in 1998. (AP/Wide World Photos)

Active Career Slugging Percentage

1.	Frank Thomas	.584
2.	Albert Belle	.577
3.	Mark McGwire	.576
4.	Mike Piazza	.575
5.	**Ken Griffey, Jr.**	**.568**
6.	Juan Gonzalez	.568
7.	Manny Ramirez	.558
8.	Barry Bonds	.556
9.	Nomar Garciaparra	.552
	Larry Walker	.552
10.	Jim Thome	.549

AL MVP Winners in the '90s

1998   Juan Gonzalez, Texas

1997   Ken Griffey, Jr., Seattle

1996   Juan Gonzalez, Texas

1995   Mo Vaughn, Boston

1994   Frank Thomas, Chicago

1993   Frank Thomas, Chicago

1992   Dennis Eckersley, Oakland

1991   Cal Ripken, Baltimore

1990   Rickey Henderson, Oakland

1998 AL MVP Voting

Player, Team	Points
Juan Gonzalez, Texas	357
Nomar Garciaparra	232
Derek Jeter	180
Mo Vaughn	135
Ken Griffey, Jr.	**135**

Active Career Leaders in Intentional Walks

Barry Bonds	289
Tony Gwynn	195
Chili Davis	181
Wade Boggs	178
Harold Baines	177
Ken Griffey, Jr.	**153**
Will Clark	150
Tim Raines	143
Darryl Strawberry	131
Fred McGriff	125

Ken slides into third with one of his 27 career triples.
(AP/Wide World Photos)

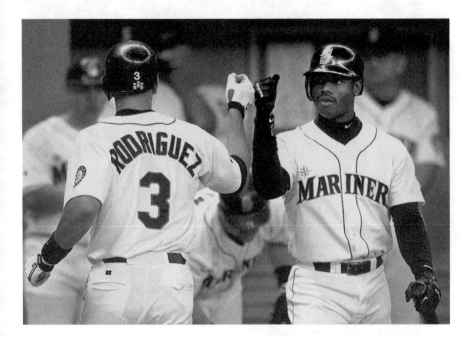

Ken and Alex Rodriguez meet between what would turn out to be back-to-back home runs at the Kingdome. (AP/Wide World Photos)

1998 American League RBI Leaders

Juan Gonzalez	157
Albert Belle	152
Ken Griffey, Jr.	**146**
Manny Ramirez	145
Alex Rodriguez	124

1998 American League HR Leaders

Ken Griffey, Jr.	**56**
Albert Belle	49
Jose Canseco	46
Juan Gonzalez	45
Manny Ramirez	45

Ken, who initially chose not to participate in the 1998 All-Star home run derby, ended up winning the contest. (AP/Wide World Photos)

1998 American League Slugging % Leaders

Albert Belle	.655
Juan Gonzalez	.630
Ken Griffey, Jr.	**.611**
Manny Ramirez	.599
Carlos Delgado	.592

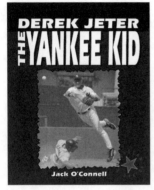

Derek Jeter:
The Yankee Kid
Author: Jack O'Connell
ISBN: 1-58261-043-6

In 1996 Derek burst onto the scene as one of the most promising young shortstops to hit the big leagues in a long time. His hitting prowess and ability to turn the double play have definitely fulfilled the early predictions of greatness.

A native of Kalamazoo, MI, Jeter has remained well grounded. He patiently signs autographs and takes time to talk to the young fans who will be eager to read more about him in this book.

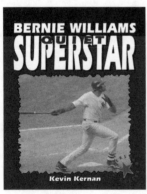

Bernie Williams:
Quiet Superstar
Author: Kevin Kernan
ISBN: 1-58261-044-4

Bernie Williams, a guitar-strumming native of Puerto Rico, is not only popular with his teammates, but is considered by top team officials to be the heir to DiMaggio and Mantle fame.

He draws frequent comparisons to Roberto Clemente, perhaps the greatest player ever from Puerto Rico. Like Clemente, Williams is humble, unassuming, and carries himself with quiet dignity. Also like Clemente, he plays with rare determination and a special elegance. He's married, and serves as a role model not only for his three children, but for his young fans here and in Puerto Rico.

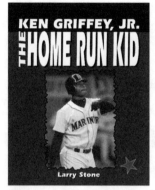

Ken Griffey, Jr.: The Home Run Kid

Author: Larry Stone
ISBN: 1-58261-041-x

Capable of hitting majestic home runs, making breathtaking catches, and speeding around the bases to beat the tag by a split second, Ken Griffey, Jr. is baseball's Michael Jordan. Amazingly, Ken reached the Major Leagues at age 19, made his first All-Star team at 20, and produced his first 100 RBI season at 21.

The son of Ken Griffey, Sr., Ken is part of the only father-son combination to play in the same outfield together in the same game, and, like Barry Bonds, he's a famous son who turned out to be a better player than his father.

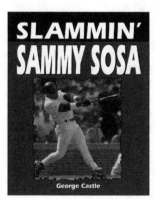

Sammy Sosa: Slammin' Sammy

Author: George Castle
ISBN: 1-58261-029-0

1998 was a break-out year for Sammy as he amassed 66 home runs, led the Chicago Cubs into the playoffs and finished the year with baseball's ultimate individual honor, MVP.

When the national spotlight was shone on Sammy during his home run chase with Mark McGwire, America got to see what a special person he is. His infectious good humor and kind heart have made him a role model across the country.

Kevin Brown:
That's Kevin with a "K"

Author: Jacqueline Salman
ISBN: 1-58261-050-9

Kevin was born in McIntyre, Georgia and played college baseball for Georgia Tech. Since then he has become one of baseball's most dominant pitchers and when on top of his game, he is virtually unhittable.

Kevin transformed the Florida Marlins and San Diego Padres into World Series contenders in consecutive seasons, and now he takes his winning attitude and talent to the Los Angeles Dodgers.

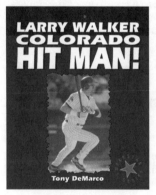

Larry Walker:
Colorado Hit Man!

Author: Tony DeMarco
ISBN: 1-58261-052-5

Growing up in Canada, Larry had his sights set on being a hockey player. He was a skater, not a slugger, but when a junior league hockey coach left him off the team in favor of his nephew, it was hockey's loss and baseball's gain.

Although the Rockies' star is known mostly for his hitting, he has won three Gold Glove awards, and has worked hard to turn himself into a complete, all-around ballplayer. Larry became the first Canadian to win the MVP award.

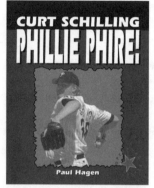

Curt Schilling: Phillie Phire!

Author: Paul Hagen
ISBN: 1-58261-055-x

Born in Anchorage, Alaska, Schilling has found a warm reception from the Philadelphia Phillies faithful. He has amassed 300+ strikeouts in the past two seasons and even holds the National League record for most strikeouts by a right handed pitcher at 319.

This book tells of the difficulties Curt faced being traded several times as a young player, and how he has been able to deal with off-the-field problems.

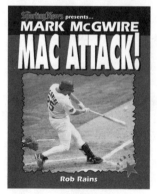

Mark McGwire: Mac Attack!

Author: Rob Rains
ISBN: 1-58261-004-5

Mac Attack! describes how McGwire overcame poor eyesight and various injuries to become one of the most revered hitters in baseball today. He quickly has become a legendary figure in St. Louis, the home to baseball legends such as Stan Musial, Lou Brock, Bob Gibson, Red Schoendienst and Ozzie Smith. McGwire thought about being a police officer growing up, but he hit a home run in his first Little League at-bat and the rest is history.

Roger Clemens: Rocket Man!

Author: Kevin Kernan
ISBN: 1-58261-128-9

Alex Rodriguez: A-plus Shortstop

ISBN: 1-58261-104-1

Baseball
SuperStar Series Titles

Collect Them All!

_____ Sandy and Roberto Alomar: Baseball Brothers

_____ Kevin Brown: Kevin with a "K"

_____ Roger Clemens: Rocket Man!

_____ Juan Gonzalez: Juan Gone!

_____ Mark Grace: Winning With Grace

_____ Ken Griffey, Jr.: The Home Run Kid

_____ Tony Gwynn: Mr. Padre

_____ Derek Jeter: The Yankee Kid

_____ Randy Johnson: Arizona Heat!

_____ Pedro Martinez: Throwing Strikes

_____ Mike Piazza: Mike and the Mets

_____ Alex Rodriguez: A-plus Shortstop

_____ Curt Schilling: Philly Phire!

_____ Sammy Sosa: Slammin' Sammy

_____ Mo Vaughn: Angel on a Mission

_____ Omar Vizquel: The Man with a Golden Glove

_____ Larry Walker: Colorado Hit Man!

_____ Bernie Williams: Quiet Superstar

_____ Mark McGwire: Mac Attack!

Available by calling 877-424-BOOK